livingnormally

Thames & Hudson

trevor naylor
photographs by niki medlik

livingnormally

where life
comes before style

with over 300
colour photographs

For Bob, Steve and Julie,
now *Living Normally* elsewhere

First published in the United Kingdom in 2007 by
Thames & Hudson Ltd, 181A High Holborn, London WC1V 7QX

www.thamesandhudson.com

British Library Cataloguing-in-Publication Data
A catalogue record for this book is available
from the British Library

ISBN-13: 978-0-500-51350-7
ISBN-10: 0-500-51350-3

Printed and bound in China

contents

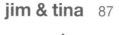

introduction the author

Welcome, do come in.

A few months ago we set off on our journey to find, pretty randomly, people who lived normally. There was no definition to follow or checklist to tick off. What was clear was that any attempt to define normal homes and lifestyles would be entirely subjective. What 'normal' means is everyone's own interpretation of what can be quite an emotive word. Some people desperately want to conform and others set out to be different. That's what is normal for them.

It was shortly after my mum's funeral that I started to ponder the meaning of home.

A child of the Thatcher era, I left school as home ownership for the majority started to be a reality; an aspiration for all then heading into the world of work and adulthood. No council house for me, I thought. I got my foot on the property ladder and have managed to go up a few rungs over time. Over the next twenty years I lived in different houses in different countries. I travelled and hung on the words of people more naturally at ease with style and fashion than a lad from Hull with limited experience, and anywhere I lived was always a place for people to visit and enjoy. My overriding concern, however, was that it looked good and that we had the 'right' sort of things in place. When travel really opened up the world to mass tourism, my flat in North London looked like a Berber tent, waiting to receive Colonel Gaddafi for mint tea, and my Sri Lankan fertility mask frightened the living wits out of anyone who came to call. It still does.

I returned to earth, however, when children and marriage arrived. The everyday demands of life when you have a family quickly override style concerns and soak up time and divert one's energies elsewhere. A show-home lifestyle is impossible for most of us.

With all this in mind, I began to reassess the ways in which our current world sells us the idea of style and the aspirations it forces upon all generations of home owners. Acres of print,

hours of TV and millions of pounds of advertising serve to idealize how our interiors should be. As I started to react against this, I wondered if a book which showed how the great people of Britain mostly live, and gave equal weight to both the homes and their inhabitants, might not be both refreshing and fun.

And so it began. Word spread quickly and enthusiasm for the project led to recommendations of people to visit. The British are not stuffy and reserved – a fact well known to the British alone, it seems – and invitations to talk and photograph houses and their occupants came in abundance. Conversation revealed that most folk prefer their homes to be welcoming to others but first and foremost need them to function in a way that suits their particular life and family grouping. Many of the photographs illustrate things that can be regarded as 'normal stuff'. These are objects and appliances that are common to almost everyone, along with ornaments (as my mum called them) that adorn

most homes and often drift along to car boot sales eventually. These are the essence of normality, for while homes come in different shapes and sizes, the things that bind them together are the things we consume.

I hope that the stars of this book are people you would like to meet sometime. All of them have differing views on life. One thing they have in common is the many bits and pieces that we all buy, and which decorate our own houses too. Increasingly, the uniformity of needs means that *Living Normally* is a completely international phenomenon, as global brands ensure we all watch the same television sets, use the same fridges and are exposed to the same cartoon characters.

That may be a depressing thought, but this book says: don't despair. There is plenty of room left for individual expression and you can see that in the pages that follow. Bear in mind that when you live normally, it's life that's the key. The rest is just stuff.

the photographer

The idea of this book immediately appealed to me, and within hours of Trevor asking me to do it, I was photographing my first house. That house was Brendan and Eileen's, which to me is the epitome of *Living Normally*. Brendan was watering his busy Lizzies in the front garden – a riot of magenta and orange that looked almost psychedelic in the evening light – when I asked his permission. I thought their house was so suitable that if he refused, I didn't think the project was worth pursuing. But they were so kind and easy-going that they gave me the keys the following day so that I could continue work while they were at the races. If this was how people were going to be, then the idea of the book was already changing. My home and background were very different from many of those I photographed, and I was now going to do my utmost to prevent my pictures from being too subjective (after all, I had just spent hours alone in Brendan and Eileen's house under the watchful eye of the Pope).

Their home was perfect for the project because it has evolved over the many years that they have lived there, paying no heed to current fashions in interiors. They have had their swimming towels for so long that they are now fashionable again and the designer living next door covets them as they hang on the washing line. Their furniture is only replaced when it breaks. The interior of their house expresses its function as a family home where all their children were born and grew up. Their lives are not hidden away or masked as they would be in a show home, and they were totally unselfconscious about being photographed. And when I interviewed them (Eileen does the talking), I learnt about life. I learnt how easy I'd had it, but only from my own questions. I also learnt how to make scones.

The book evolved into something that was more about the people that lived in the houses than the interiors themselves, and unlike those

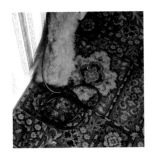

in conventional style books and magazines, some of the shots have people in them. Similarly, the photos were not staged: I wanted to show people's lives as they really are, and resisted even the tiniest tweak of a knick-knack into a more aesthetic position.

Brendan and Eileen were among the easiest to interview. Sometimes I wasn't sure what questions to ask. Once I asked someone (not in the book, as it turned out) if his flat felt like 'home', and his fascinating responses started me thinking about whether my house was a home. Although this upset my partner, it did at least prompt him to paint the bedroom.

I also learnt that style and all its trappings can get in the way of feeling 'at home'. The Buddhist community had such an atmosphere of calm that I didn't want to leave, and one of the women told me she felt a lot more at home there than in the stylish flat she had once owned, where she had been so concerned with things looking right that she had been unable to just 'be'. And so I began to consider happiness.

Those with no concern for what the neighbours might think laughed so loudly together that I could hear them before I got to their front door.

The project has suggested to me that there is no such thing as 'normal'. It also showed me that there is a way of living that makes you a lot happier than if you're constantly worrying about your paintwork or whether you've done the washing-up when you have an unexpected visitor. After all, you can always imitate Sarah when visitors cross your threshold: just ply them with so much alcohol that they won't notice....

brendan & eileen

Enjoying their retirement, this devoted couple are often away visiting their children, but when at home they are invaluable to their church, swim at the local lido, and love a good day out at the races.

Brendan and Eileen have lived in this house for nearly fifty years. The house reflects that time, not as a museum set in the past but as a mirror of their time together, as parents and now as retirees. Brendan came over from Ireland in 1958, Eileen shortly afterwards, and they married in 1959. Brendan was a bus driver and conductor, and Eileen worked as a childminder.

The house has a warmth that envelops you; everything in it is beautifully kept and the objects are clearly things with personal meaning for Brendan and Eileen. The smell of baking cakes is a regular element of home life. Their devotion to their faith is quietly displayed on walls and mantelpieces, but no more than that. They are committed to it and much of their social life revolves round activities at their local church and community centre.

As parents they take their responsibilities seriously. The pride and love inherent in the family photographs is clear; in some rooms they are the dominant feature. They have five children of their own and a mounting number of grandchildren to think about.

They are enjoying the time they now have together to relax and to garden. Eileen is very house-proud and keeps the place looking nice for the regular visitors who come to share a cup of tea or for the weekends when family come by. They love to swim every day (weather permitting) at the local lido, one of the few that stay open all year round.

While they are close to their church, they have other interests too, not least of which is the traditional Irish love of horseracing. They enjoy a little flutter on the ponies, especially for the big races like the Derby, and like to get to meetings whenever they can.

Brendan and Eileen have life sorted. They give as much back, if not more, than they receive, while still enjoying themselves. They have raised a family and kept a successful relationship alive for nearly fifty years and see each day to come as time to have fun and do something useful. Good for them.

above On a cold night, gas fires like this one heat the room really quickly.
opposite Brendan ties his shoelaces for his daily 10 a.m. stroll around the block. The photos on the walls are of their own children, and all the others Eileen has devotedly childminded over the years.

opposite above left   Mug trees are a neat idea. The mugs are family gifts for the 'World's Best Granny'.
opposite above, centre   Eileen keeps everything neat and tidy.

opposite above right   Brendan and Eileen are committed to their local church.
opposite below   Eileen bakes some scones in the kitchen. One of the few things they have done

to update their house is to insert a larger window over the sink, to let a bit more light in.
below   Brendan dozes in front of the TV.

above The grandchildren are always welcome in the house, with toys and books ready for them. Sometimes there are so many staying that there are two children to a bed, but this just adds to the fun, with Grandma chasing them and growling till the little ones squeal.

above This is where Brendan and Eileen conceived
three of their children. The same bed has lasted for
over twenty years, and they never replace any furniture
if it's still in one piece.

opposite Who cares about the big ideas? It's the
little things that really make a home special to you.

above Brendan and Eileen's swimming things on the
line after a day at the lido.

james & steve

A couple who keep their place in good shape because it feels better that way, and who don't take style too seriously. There's no need to be afraid as you enter the Hallway of Horror....

James and Steve love their flat so much that they prefer to stay in as much as they can. They have lived in the flat for nine years. When they first looked at this place, James in particular disliked it, especially the side passage which has now been turned into their secret garden. James and Steve are very house-proud, and have even started learning about gardening since they began living here together. As well as adoring their flat they are also very much in love and happily admit to having become 'homebodies' in their mid-thirties.

Another reason for their stay-at-home attitude is James's MS. During his last bout, he could do nothing but sit on the sofa and watch TV, while gazing at the unfinished decorating. They both realized that this added to James's illness, so when he felt better, they finished it all off and also got rid of a lot of unwanted clutter.

The space is dual-purpose. James works at home during the day in a corner of the living room, but each evening the flat becomes a home once again.

The flat is a collection of new and old, with furniture collected from relatives or bought second-hand. Things they particularly like are the leather drinks cabinet, which Steve picked up at a junk shop near his work in Waterloo, and the timeless elegance of the unusual blue leather Chesterfield. Dotted around the home are objects and pictures from their childhoods, including the picture of a train station which had been in James's room when he was a boy. James admits to liking kitsch more than Steve does, but by and large they have similar tastes and agree about what they like.

Although it has taken time to get the place as they want it, they now feel very settled and happy in a space that really belongs to them.

above left The cocktail cabinet in the sitting room.
below Humorous details in the bathroom.
opposite It took some nerve for the boys to radically change their fantastic hallway from pale pink to deep green, but it worked! The pictures are all stills from horror movies.

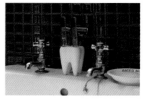

above Who says men can't get themselves organized? Here boys' toys look fabulous.

opposite When space has to be used for both work and pleasure, you have to find a balance that is successful seven days a week. Steve and James show they can do that and keep their sense of style.

sarah, lizzie, anne sasha, nell & ted

Single mother Sarah has got her priorities right. 'Life's too short for cleaning,' she says as she pours herself another glass of sherry. And her five happy, sorted kids are living proof that mother knows best.

'Houses are rather like lovers. There has to be something to attract you in the first place, so you don't mind when things go wrong.'

Sarah's house is her own. She bought it hurriedly while in the middle of a divorce, ignoring lots of well-meaning advice because she simply couldn't bear the idea of buying a modern house: 'characterless boxes', she calls them. She had an idea of the kind of house she wanted and when she saw that this one was for sale, she simply knocked on the door, looked around and instantly knew it was the place for her. She says: 'Houses are rather like lovers. There has to be something to attract you in the first place, so you don't mind when things go wrong.'

Sarah has two dining tables: one to eat off and one for her family's artwork. This is because when Sarah was a child she remembers having to move her homework in order to eat and she didn't want to inflict that on her children.

Although the house is big, Sarah and her five children have managed to fill it with junk they just can't get rid of. They have lots of books which she regards as a security blanket of information. Sarah happily admits to being not very good at tidying, and sees her hobbies as much more important than cleaning the house. When she does start cleaning, the first question the children ask is 'Who's coming round?'

The kids contribute more to the mess than to the organization, with the twins' bedroom in particular looking like an explosion in a clothes factory. But Sarah's attitude is that it's their room, so they can deal with it. As the children get older, they do more to keep their rooms in order. She does despair sometimes at the chaos her brood create but knows she will miss them when they grow up and leave home.

Ultimately Sarah sees her home as a space for living and being and doing, not as an end in itself. Her own mother despaired of her, feeling she had brought Sarah up to do things properly, and both Sarah's sisters do therapeutic vacuuming, so Sarah believes she missed out on the tidiness gene. It is perhaps ironic that her first job after university was as a housekeeper to a gay millionaire in the south of France. But Sarah thinks a house only needs to be comfortable enough to visit, although she does wonder if her friends come because she plies them with alcohol so they don't notice the mess.

Sarah fails to see why a fear of messing up the place should stop you from being creative. 'The houses you see in Sunday supplements suggest the owners don't do anything,' she says. 'Otherwise, why would it all be so clean and untouched?'

And after the children move on? 'Bring on the grandchildren and the Playdough,' she says. 'I don't want the kids to say that all I ever did was moan at them about leaving their stuff around.'

above Family photos are what most people would choose to save if the house were on fire.

previous pages
Sarah on tidy kids: 'Boys don't seem to care too much about their surroundings. They are far too interested in what food is on offer.'

The floor of the hall is a great place to play, and in this house it's often full of teenagers because it's home to the Playstation.

sarah, lizzie, anne, sasha, nell & ted

Sarah's dedication to free expression in her children's early years has not stopped them growing into tidier teenagers. Her eldest son Ted, who has now left home and gone to university, used to do all the vacuuming when visitors were expected. The others have not, however, progressed to the ultimate test of doing their own laundry, as we see in Sarah's room (opposite).

roger & mary

Two families came together under this roof. Now Roger and Mary look forward to retirement and to spending as much time in their caravan as possible. They believe in seeing the world while they still feel young and strong.

Roger and Mary came together some time after losing their partners in sad circumstances. Roger's wife died suddenly after an illness and Mary's husband was killed in a car accident. Both had two children and found themselves as the carer and breadwinner in one. They bought this large house in 1984 when they got married, and it became the successful space in which they brought up four boys together, all of whom now have grown up and left the nest.

With this history, it's no surprise that they felt strongly that the house had to be for family first. The dining table where we sat and talked is the place where all major family decisions have been made. They say that when guests come for dinner it seems impossible to leave the table to sit in the lounge, and that people find it hard to pry themselves away at the end of the evening. As the boys grew up, it was a rule that the family sit and eat together, and over dinner or Sunday lunch everything was up for debate. There were no taboos and every topic from girls to drugs to sex education was discussed at table.

It's easy to imagine arriving in this house and not leaving. Nonetheless, Roger and Mary face the thought of leaving themselves now that the boys have gone. Mary in particular dreads the idea, although they know the day must come.

Roger and Mary don't watch much TV and they prefer their own music to the radio much of the time. They do, however, have views on what a home should be. 'A show house is just that, a house for show. It's not a home,' says Roger. They believe they passed this attitude on to their children, who have their own places and families now. However, they also recognize that buying a home as an investment is more in people's minds these days. 'We never thought for a minute whether this house would grow in value when we bought it. We never imagined leaving it really,' says Mary. 'But one of our boys has just bought a place and it's part of a five-year plan.'

Caravanning is something they love and they travel extensively. 'When we were younger, travel was not an option most of the time,' they say, 'but nowadays everyone does it.' So do they. Their longest road trip was a sixteen-week tour of Europe, taking them to the very top of Norway. 'We will travel a lot while we can,' was their joint view of active retirement. Both have worked in education for many years, with Mary also working towards being a lay preacher.

The postcards that cover the fridge are the brightest things in the house, adding a shock of colour to the kitchen. They like to keep their memories of their journeys around them, and also enjoy wines from France, a place they love to be. Also on display is a gift from a grateful caravanner whom they helped when they passed his stricken van on the road in Brittany.

Roger and Mary have been lucky enough to find two happy marriages in their lives, and their time together has been fun. What lies ahead looks even more enjoyable and a fair reward for difficult times past.

right The table is still the place for family business and communal eating.
below Roger and Mary work in education and do lots of work at home. The rise of the home office makes this an increasingly common sight.

Mary in her kitchen. The postcards on the fridge tell the story of family travels. When they sell up and move on, the fridge may stay put, but the postcards will come along.

Many other things in the house have been picked up on Roger and Mary's travels. They love the painting of lavender fields in particular and the bottle of pastis is also a favourite French souvenir.

opposite above What the design historians of the future might call late 20th-century chic.
opposite below Spare rooms can seem lonely places until visitors arrive to bring them energy.
below Exercise equipment is a common feature in modern homes. Its relative position in the home often indicates its level of usage.

'A show house is just that,
a house for show.
It's not a home.'

shaun, boxy & boo

Shaun is an Irish builder who lives a life of true impermanence as he regularly moves house, depending on his current building project. In fact, this particular house was due to be knocked down the day after these photographs were taken.

Shaun is an Irish builder who lives with his lodger, Boxy, and his dog, Boo. He is happy living anywhere and is a tidy and organized person who loves keep himself busy. Despite recently giving up smoking and drinking, Shaun has maintained his relaxed nature and likes being part of the community wherever he happens to be working.

The house and its decor reflect the fact that wherever Shaun lives, he is never far away from moving, but while this would be unsettling for most, he is quite happy.

However laid back he is, he does still need to have a few rooms that are homely and decorated with his favourite bits and pieces, most of which have some sentimental value. Another key is that there is always a room ready wherever he lives so that his daughter Adele can come to stay. Otherwise, he lives and works one day at a time, always asks people how they are,

and is generally content. 'I am always all right,' he says, which is usually true, apart from the time he fell off a roof and fractured his spine. Then there was much concern from the (mostly female) neighbours he knows up and down the street. Shaun hated being inactive while he got better; that, for him, is not normal.

His favourite getaway is the Dominican Republic, where he goes regularly to chill out, and where he can let his body recover from the rigours of construction work.

opposite Boo waits in the hall for Shaun to come home from the building site. The ground floor was left relatively unfurnished so that any unwanted visitors would think the house was uninhabited.

PENGUIN
BOOKS

THE GARDEN
PARTY

KATHERINE
MANSFIELD

trevor, liz, gwynnie & robbie

Proof that living in a timber-framed listed cottage and running a business from home can conflict with the practical necessities of bringing up a young family.

This house is, on the face of it, the perfect rural idyll: a 14th-century house with a twinkling Dickensian-style bookshop at the front and an enclosed garden at the back. Living normally? Not quite for the owners of this mixed-up property, who came to enjoy a love–hate relationship with the building that was both home and workplace.

It's not unusual to pop into a local shop and find that the family who own the store also live on the premises; you may even get a tantalizing glimpse of what lies through the door behind the counter. But have you ever considered what it means for the people who live and work there?

The advantages are obvious enough; no commuting and no expensive lunches as you can always eat from your own kitchen. But the downsides are plentiful too. The hours are often long, living over the shop can create security issues, and, unless you are quite lucky, the location means that children are living away from their friends. For us, however (and this is your humble author speaking), the thing that made us fall out of love with the experience was

the fact that you rarely escape the business and time off only exists if you go away on holiday (and even then, someone has to mind the shop).

Modern living is also difficult in period buildings, with everything from satellite TV to the internet requiring either planning permission or specialist wiring. But it's children who find such a home hardest to enjoy; sloping floors and lime plaster walls mean games are hard to play and posters are impossible. Even bedroom trampolining is outlawed as it brings the living-room ceiling down! All this and only having your parents around on a Sunday meant that Robbie and Gwynnie did not get enough quality time with Mum and Dad and sleepovers were not easy due to lack of space.

It was a lovely house, packed with loads of things, and chickens too, but we had to accept that it did not work for us. I hope the photos show it was a home that was loved, but since this book came into being we have moved to a square-walled, flat-floored box in a cul-de-sac with leylandii around the garden and we all love it. That feels like living normally to us.

above With the door through to the shop firmly closed, the living area becomes a haven of peace for family time on Sundays.

above The makeshift 'wardrobe', a short-term
solution that lasted ten years. The put-up bed is
there for Grandpa's visits, or kids' sleepovers.

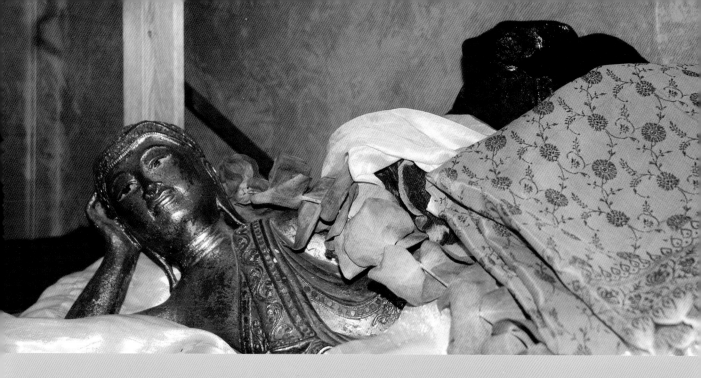

jenny, diana, shantidevi, rebecca & karunamati

There are times in our lives when we may find ourselves sharing a home with strangers. This Buddhist community welcomes people to share more than the contents of the fridge.

This house became a Buddhist community eight years ago when five artists moved in. It has evolved as women come and go, and being an artist is not a precondition for joining, although the house's Buddhist name *Lalitanivasa* literally means 'abode of artistic playfulness'.

While it has always been an exclusively female group, the current householders say it would not be impossible for a man to come and live there, provided that everyone in the group discussed and agreed to it. Housekeeping is a shared task and they are fortunate that the current mix of women have different preferences and choose to wash up, clean, cook, vacuum or work in the garden, so life runs pretty smoothly.

In short, the team play to their strengths and both work and relax together when their schedules coincide. They shop communally, and eat as a whole group once a week; otherwise it's as and when they are in the house at the same time. More recently texting has made co-ordination much easier.

They are an international group of single people so the concept of whether this was a home or not was crucial. They feel the house has a lovely atmosphere partly because of the Buddhist aura that permeates it. Kindness and generosity are central elements of Buddhism; combined with a strong ecological message about preserving life and recycling, this makes for a home where nothing but light and joy can be the order of the day.

Community life challenges ego and makes you think about the things that really matter: sharing and caring for each other and being part of a team. The women try to share thoughts and feelings and live honestly and openly together in a mutually supportive way.

May all beings
be well
May all beings
be happy
May all beings
be free from
suffering

above Contemplation can take many forms.

The make-up of the household is different at different times of the day, meaning an ever-changing mix of people that almost removes the need for a social life outside the community.

Of course, the team have outside interests and friends, but you get the feeling that most of what they need as human beings can be found within the community walls.

The shrine room. Each resident has their own area within it for meditation and contemplation.

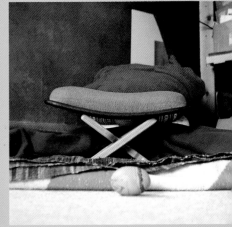

Each bedroom also has its own shrine, which the women create themselves. Sometimes these look incongruous in a room full of modern objects.

evelyn, wayne & kevin

This Caribbean lady looks younger each
year as she strolls through life in a relaxed
fashion. She lives happily in her house,
a slice of island life in England.

Evelyn looks much younger than she really is. Her secret, she claims, is that she doesn't stress about anything. A great way to be, but all the more admirable in Evelyn's case, since her life has not always been easy. The contrast between this and Evelyn's original home in St Vincent could not be more stark and it has taken her years to decide that she prefers England. Perhaps her love of snow tipped the balance.

She came to England in 1969; her husband was already here and sent for her to join him. He was not at the airport to meet her when she arrived, but fortunately someone she met on the plane helped her to find him. It turned out that he was ill and at a friend's house. She did not like London at first; it was winter and she thought the trees had all died until her husband explained that they came back to life in the spring. She was also upset at the way people closed their doors, when the houses in St Vincent were left open all the time.

Evelyn's husband died in 2004. He had come to England as a sailor and when they met he was already married and had a son, Kevin, who is now fifty and still lives with Evelyn, along with another son, Wayne. Evelyn has eleven children in total, now grown up but not too far away to visit. She has lived in this house for twenty-three years, and is a Muslim although her children are all Catholics like their father was.

Sundays are the most special time, and cooking is at the centre of the day for those who come by. Traditional Caribbean food is always a draw and Evelyn loves being at the heart of the action. The house has a strong Caribbean influence. I once attended a wedding in St Vincent and this house is a little slice of the island here in Britain. It has a sense of place and confidence that ensures everyone feels instantly at home.

Evelyn has managed the important trick of keeping close to her origins while embracing her new country. She keeps her relaxed vibe by focusing on what matters to her most: loving her family and finding time for friends. Big families are traditional in many cultures; each generation cares for the previous one as they grow older and the momentum of many lives helps to ensure everyone gets looked after and looked out for. That's Evelyn's style of 'living normally'.

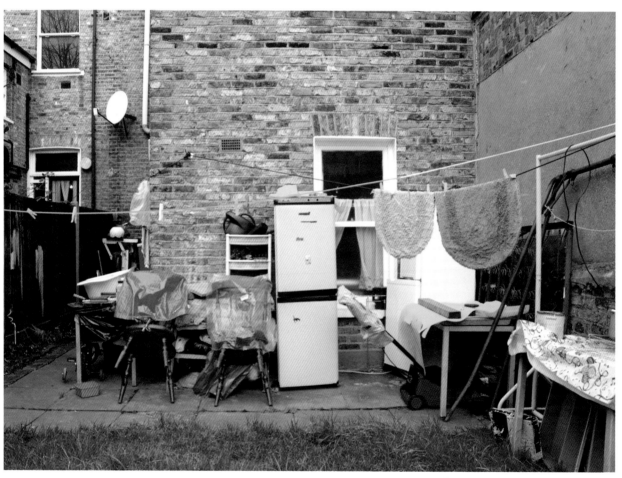

opposite The garden is an outdoor space to enjoy
and party in, and includes a big wooden stage where
all the grandchildren get together and make lots of
noise. When it snows, they all run out and play.

below The kitchen was painted in sunny colours by
Evelyn's daughter. Evelyn cooks traditional Caribbean
food in here, and all the family come round for big
Sunday dinners.

Evelyn's home preserves a slice
of Caribbean life in England.

tessa, jack, bradley, chris, craig & ross

This house is surprisingly clean and tidy for six music students, but the broken windows, empty beer bottles and the remains of last night's kebab give its occupants away.

'It's a night house. You can smell curry at 3 a.m.'

The idea of the typical student house was exaggerated in the public consciousness by the crazed and slightly psychopathic TV series *The Young Ones*, where the property in question was merely a backdrop to the wild lives and misguided opinions of its inhabitants. Tessa and the five boys she shares with are all music students, but their attitudes to this house and their family homes are less extreme than the TV stereotype and suggest that the nesting instinct comes early in life for some.

Tessa and all her housemates are living away from their home towns, and it seems that home stays with them as they live in this more transient environment. Jack misses the sea now he is nearer to London. 'Everything I did was about the beach,' he says. 'Around here, everyone goes to the park for their space.'

People who live in a shared space often feel that they need a place to escape to where they can really be themselves. Given that Jack offered Tessa £50 for her bed because his room is so small that he can't bring girls back, it seems he has some space issues. Tessa has the bedroom that feels the most homely, yet she is rarely there. She spends most of her time at her boyfriend's place – 'shagging', say the guys – and so is not around much. She also claims: 'I do get a lot of sexual harassment being the only girl – arse-slapping, grabbing, licking, biting.'

She says of the house: 'I love it because there is always someone around. It's never an empty house. Everyone is up to their own thing. It's a night house. You can smell curry at three in the morning and stuff like that. Random.'

In general, these students seem to rub along well and take most elements of property care as seriously as is needed. Inevitably, six people with no long-term financial or emotional investment in a place will mean a house that is no more than a convenient place to be. As Tessa says: 'We are just living a student life. It's not going to be like this forever. One day I will grow up and get a home of my own, which will be very different.'

opposite It's obvious which room is Tessa's (although she rarely ever sleeps in it) because of its neatness and femininity.

above Bradley's room.
The boys' rooms reveal their musical interests – Craig's equipment (opposite below right) shows the most contemporary side of his chosen career path.

jim & tina

The house with secrets in the loft, which we were not allowed to photograph. But let's just say that Jim's army training and Tina's fondness for all things military could be a clue.

This modern home might be described as military chic – high tech, yes, but with nice touches of sentiment and fun. Evidence of the couple's army past combine with family memories and the flat-screen technology that is changing the face of modern homes.

above One of a number of televisions in the household, this one is positioned above Jim's knives and iPod dock and is perfect for watching his favourite programme, *South Park*.

opposite above Jim is the only tree surgeon in his company who cleans his boots, and he does so every week. He undoubtedly also has the cleanest kitchen floor in the company!

opposite below right Tina's prized possession is her Royal Air Force Pilot commission in pride of place on the wall in the hall. If the house burned down, this is what she would try to rescue.

ivy

Ivy doesn't make a big song and dance about life, which is a surprise since hers has been full of music and the stage. A big family and a larger-than-life husband complete the picture of a home that packs more into a council house than you might believe.

These days Ivy lives by herself, but she is not on her own much – her six children and numerous grandchildren ensure she doesn't get lonely.

It's not long since Albert, her husband of over fifty years, passed away and at once she lost both her life partner and stage partner. A former guardsman and police constable who played the spoons, Albert had joined his wife on stage when he retired and together they ran the 'Wrinklies Road Show', touring nursing homes and sheltered accommodation, performing for fun and raising money for charity. Well-known locally for many years, Ivy and Albert also had a taste of national stardom when they appeared to great acclaim on ITV with Michael Barrymore.

Ivy's house has always attracted people to it. Her house parties at Christmas or New Year were a magnet for family, friends and neighbours, although sadly 'Blondie's Bar' is now in storage as the house has recently had some major makeover work. The lounge area has been transformed, partly because Ivy could not bear to live with the constant memory of her beloved Albert; the loss and pain were just too much for her. The coloured walls she now enjoys would not have been allowed in Albert's day, she tells me. 'He would never have anything but white or cream on the walls.' The decoration continues into the kitchen, where a comfortable chair allows conversation with Ivy when she cooks, or while someone does it for her. It's a very amiable place to be.

The house is stuffed with memories and objects that portray family life and the successes of Ivy, Albert, their children and grandchildren. Once the kids had left home, Ivy and Albert got seriously interested in sun-seeking, a tale told in the collection of fridge magnets.

Recently Ivy went on holiday and while she was away, the family got together and carried out a major makeover of the garden. Nicknamed 'Ground Farce', the operation took a huge amount of effort but the result is a wonderful haven for Ivy to sit in and enjoy now that she is not allowed to spend much time out in the sun. Like much of the house, it is a warm combination of modern ideas and fun items designed to raise a smile.

Ivy strongly feels that a house should be a home, and that family happiness comes first. In this regard, Ivy and Albert's attitudes have been

below The living room has been given a touch of colour for the first time in Ivy's married life.

carried through to their own children. Together the family are a solid and powerful team who watch out for one another.

Ivy and Albert had a tough start in life, both starting work at the age of fourteen after wartime evacuation. Ivy had a job handfeeding metal sheets into a machine that made Brasso tins and Albert worked in a coal mine. Perhaps this is why they did so much to ensure that their home was a safe and happy place to grow up.

above The kitchen and dining area is small but full of things to look at. The fridge magnets represent Ivy's travels and those of her many children and grandchildren.

right The bathroom tiles are brightened by rose stickers – another touch added by Ivy after Albert's death.

opposite centre left Cuttings in a clipframe, commemorating Albert and Ivy's appearance on Michael Barrymore's TV show.

opposite centre right The Spillbuster, a classic piece of 1970s design for vacuuming up those table crumbs.

opposite below right Family photographs on the stairs, including Ivy's party after the family gave her garden a surprise makeover.

above The spare room is an ideal place for things Ivy cannot bear to part with, and a welcoming space for friends and family if they come to stay.

overleaf Ivy's garden, as transformed by Operation 'Ground Farce'.

below Albert was a lifelong rugby fan.

pete, sue & max

Pete and Sue love living in their mobile home in the country. He listens to the dawn chorus as he lies in bed, thankful he no longer works as a dustman. Her cross-stitch pictures are now of birds and flowers, not the street scenes from her days in town.

Space in a mobile home is limited, but it's enough for Pete and Sue because they love the location so much. Everything in their home is precious or practical. Most important of all is Max the cat, as they were told they had to get rid of their beloved dog, Jack, soon after they moved into the park, which broke Pete's heart.

The pictures on the walls (top) have all been created by Sue, who sits at the window stitching intricate designs and knitting miniature doll's clothes using cocktail sticks as needles. The subject matter of her pictures has changed since they moved from the town to the country.

opposite below The couple collect frogs in every shape and form.

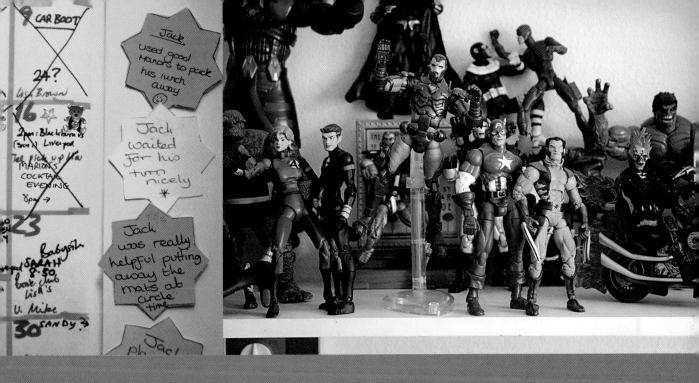

terry, ailish, jack & leo

Charity shop bargains and action figures
are just a backdrop to this creative home
dedicated to family life and fun. Prepare
to dine with Daleks and meet the kids.

Ailish and Terry share many views, particularly about the need for time alone, away from the hectic routine of daily life. For Terry this means time in his study, a place where he also works – he is a teacher, which involves preparation at home. However, the study also holds other secrets. Terry has an extensive collection of action figures, with a strong emphasis on James Bond and his treasured *Doctor Who* collection, along with the occasional superhero or villain. He has been collecting for many years, going right back to his childhood. The study is now quite full and his concept of DIY extends only to how much room he can save by moving Blofeld closer to Bond. Terry believes his collecting habit is typical of an only child, but claims he is growing out of his addiction to time alone as family life takes over.

Ailish's most-loved room is the bedroom she shares with her husband, which she regards as

her sanctuary away from the kids she adores but who fill her day from early morning till night. The bedroom is a place for her and Terry to be together too, of course, and decorating it was very much a joint project. It's a place where she reads, drinks tea, and comes to a stop.

Ailish herself had quite an unusual childhood and now she wants to fill this home with joy and happiness for her kids, providing them with a stable base as they grow up. She went to eight different primary schools and lived in as many houses before the age of eleven, so the idea of one real home for her children, her husband and herself is terribly important to her.

opposite left Terry's room.
opposite right The dining table in the hall.
left and below Ailish works hard as a mum but is
also an illustrator with ambition. The garage is her
space, and all her materials are carefully sorted and
labelled for easy access, should she have half an hour
to herself.

above and opposite Terry's collection is on display in his room. He is a teacher, so the room doubles as a study.

overleaf The rest of the house is dedicated to bringing up Jack and Leo in a creative atmosphere. Jack is Superman. I know because he told me so.

vikram

Vikram enjoys his own company. His perfect weekend is spent lying on the floor listening to cricket on the World Service. His mother wishes he would meet a nice girl and settle down, but he fears she'd object to him cleaning his bicycle on the living-room carpet.

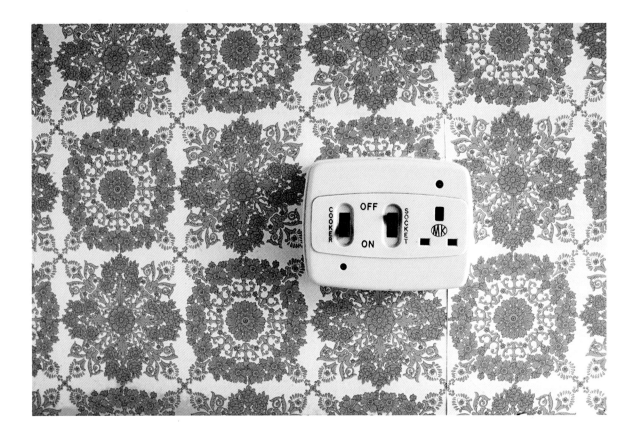

'There's nothing more boring than when my mates start discussing DIY. Then it's time to leave the pub.'

Vikram lives in a block of flats built in the 1970s, and the cooker, electrical sockets and decoration are relics of that decade. Most of the furniture in the flat is inherited, and the kitchen wallpaper is from the old lady who lived in the flat before him. He has lived here for over ten years and can see no point in updating it or getting more contemporary furniture, as what he has is comfortable enough.

The glass front of the cooker (opposite) is shattered from the time that Vikram lost his patience with the timer, which refused to be switched off, and hit it with a hammer.

vicky, daniel & jonathan

Vicky has been collecting since she was a child. Her eclectic taste has transcended all trends in antiques, creating an environment that is both unique and witty.

Vicky is an art teacher who lives alone in her house since her sons Daniel and Jonathan left home for university and art college. Unlike most parents, however, she still keeps a room that is most definitely their space for whenever they come back and stay. We all remember the day when our parents changed the use of our bedrooms, pulled down those tacked-up posters, and painted the walls magnolia. Not Vicky. But she has clear ideas about design and what looks good in her home. And Daniel's door covered in flyers makes a great juxtaposition with the mannequin on the upstairs landing with an 'Upper Class' ticket tucked into its cleavage.

Vicky started collecting things when she was a child. Her father took her and her siblings to jumble sales for entertainment, because they couldn't afford a TV. But Vicky was the only child in her family who really took to this. She has been acquiring the things that are now in her house ever since those days. When she went to art college, she moved into a huge flat in London's Little Venice that she somehow managed to get for a cheap rent. This was perfect for her hobby because of its proximity to the excellent local antique markets. There she picked up all sorts of bargain antiques that were not currently fashionable, as her tastes were consistent and not swayed by current trends – an imperative for 'living normally'.

Things were difficult for Vicky when she eventually moved from the flat, as its vast rooms had easily accommodated her acquisitions, and she found herself having to compromise as motherhood meant that she and her then-husband moved to this house, with its smaller rooms, in the catchment area for good schools.

She still misses London and that first flat, which she really felt to be home, but she makes the most of the car-boot sales in the suburbs. She has so much fantastic stuff that she uses a rotational system, swapping the things in the house with those stored in the loft and garage. She can even forget about much-loved objects until they are rediscovered and she rearranges the shelves with her inimitable taste and wit.

above left Vicky's eye for detail and her own unique style extends to the plant-holders in the garden.

With two boys growing up in this house, the Queen has had a lot more to look at over the years than just a collection of antique egg cups. Vicky was nervous about painting the staircase walls in such a cold, conventional grey, but with her fascinating collection of possessions in place, the final effect is far from dull.

Vicky is an art teacher, and her eye for interesting objects is obvious around her house. The fruit-bowl statue (opposite) and the bust (below) are two of Vicky's favourite possessions, and rarely get relegated to the loft or garage.

opposite Computers have become all-pervasive but most homes find space for them somehow.

above and overleaf A place for everything and everything in its place, even if it means sleeping in the cellar.

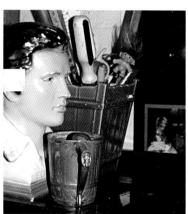

author's acknowledgments
To Niki, who took the ball and ran with it.

photographer's acknowledgments
A big thank you to Tim.
To Sophy, Alison and Ailish for all their help and encouragement.
To John Gollings for his endless advice and generosity in
showing me how it's done.
To Trevor for all the laughs.
And to the stars of this book, for welcoming me into their homes.